A Kid's Life in
ANCIENT
EGYPT

by

Hermione Redshaw

BEARPORT
PUBLISHING

Minneapolis, Minnesota

Credits:
All images are courtesy of Shutterstock.com, unless otherwise specified. With thanks to Getty Images, Thinkstock Photo, and iStockphoto. Recurring images – YamabikaY, Tartila, TADDEUS, sumkinn, Vlada Young, Gaidamashchuk, pics five, Andrey_Kuzmin, Macrovector, Jemastock, Milano M, Oligo22, ONYXprj. Cover – Fedor Selivanov, Marti Bug Catcher, Kabardins photo. 2–3 – Gordana Adzieva. 4–5 – donatas1205, AlexAnton, New Africa, angizzz, VaLiza. 6–7 – Alfmaler, Krakenimages.com, Lapina, Marco Ossino, Merydolla, Mind Pixell. 8–9 – 4 PM production, Everilda, Olga Kuevda, robuart, RHJPhtotos, SIRNARM USAVICH. 10–11 – BearFotos, Dmytro Buianskyi, Jaroslav Moravcik. 12–13 – Dunhill, Ievgenii Meyer, MasaMima, matryoshka, Matyas Rehak, Phakorn Kasikij, Quintanilla. 14–15 – bildfokus.se, Litvalifa, Monkey Business Images, SpicyTruffel, tan_tan, Victoria Sergeeva. 16–17 – Evil Panda (Wikimedia Commons), Hogan Imaging, matryoshka, Nomad_Soul, Paul Vinten, Valadzionak Volha. 18–19 – Captmondo (WikimediaCommons), grmarc, Macrovector, NotionPic, Olena Brodetska, Radiokafka. 20–21 – Beatrice Barberis, Creativa Images, Einsamer Schütze (Wikimedia Commons), Kateryna Onyshchuk, Oscar Peralta Anechina, Perfect_kebab. 22–23 – BNP Design Studio, Body Stock, matryoshka, GoodStudio, Red Fox studio. 24–25 – amelipulen, Anastasiia Kulikovska, Mega Pixel, Photick. 26–27 – amelipulen, ESB Professional, matryoshka, pink.mousy, Prostock-studio. 28–29 – GolF2532, gualtiero boffi, Laboo Studio, nattanan726, NotionPic, OlegDoroshin, Olga Kuevda. 30 – VaLiza.

Library of Congress Cataloging-in-Publication Data is available at www.loc.gov or upon request from the publisher.

ISBN: 979-8-88509-953-0 (hardcover)
ISBN: 979-8-88822-127-3 (paperback)
ISBN: 979-8-88822-273-7 (ebook)

© 2024 BookLife Publishing
This edition is published by arrangement with BookLife Publishing.

For more information, write to Bearport Publishing, 5357 Penn Avenue South, Minneapolis, MN 55419.

Contents

Money In and Out

That new video game is finally for sale! It costs $40, and you made $50 doing chores. However, you need to buy a new backpack for school. You want to see a movie with your friends, too. How will you pay for it all? The answer is **budgeting**.

Most people get their money from working. You may earn money from weekend jobs. Or you could do chores at home or for people you know.

CONTENTS

Being a KID

It's tough being a kid. A bad haircut can ruin your week. Teachers keep giving you homework. And your parents are always telling you to share.

But how hard is it, really? If you think being a kid is tough today, imagine what it was like living as a kid in ancient Egypt!

Your textbooks would be written in pictures and you'd have to share a bedroom with your entire family. You'd even have to wear your hair shaved on one side. That's tough!

ANCIENT EGYPT

Get ready to travel back in time and see what life was like for kids in ancient Egypt.

Ancient EGYPT

Ancient Egypt formed about 5,000 years ago. This **civilization** was known for inventing and building amazing things, including the pyramids. Many of these structures can still be seen in Egypt today.

Thanks for the fresh breath, ancient Egyptians!

The ancient Egyptians created one of the first written languages and even made the paper to write it on. We also have them to thank for toothpaste.

This is harder than a jigsaw puzzle!

Some of their inventions were quite different in ancient times than they are today. Paper didn't come in notebooks. Instead, it was often rolled in **scrolls**. Ancient Egyptian paper was **woven** from thin pieces of a plant called papyrus.

This toothpaste is a little sharp!

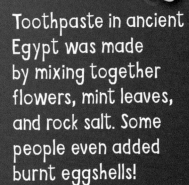

Toothpaste in ancient Egypt was made by mixing together flowers, mint leaves, and rock salt. Some people even added burnt eggshells!

SURVIVING
the Time

Surviving childhood might seem easy. Your parents give you food and a warm home. Doctors help if you're sick. However, growing up in ancient Egypt was a whole different game!

It sounds like the Egyptians were playing life on hard mode!

As many as half of ancient Egypt's children might not have lived past their first birthdays. Many **diseases** that we can easily treat today were deadly in ancient Egypt.

It's my first birthday next week!

Some of the earliest written information about **medicine** came from ancient Egypt. However, it didn't include vaccines or high-tech treatments. Many doctors at the time relied on **natural** medicines made from plants.

Getting sick wasn't the only thing to watch out for. Ancient Egypt was home to lots of scorpions and snakes. A simple bandage wouldn't be enough if you met one of those!

Hey! Watch where you're walking!

FAMILY Is Forever

Living with your family under one roof can feel pretty crowded when you've got a large family—like those in ancient Egypt!

We need to fit her on the sofa, too!

Family is forever—there's no escape!

Even after children got married, they didn't always leave home. They may live with all of their brothers, sisters, aunts, uncles, and cousins for the rest of their lives!

Kids in ancient Egypt were sometimes called the staff of their father's old age. That means a child had to help their father as he got older. Even if you moved away from home, you'd have to head back whenever Dad needed help!

Son, I need your help.

Son, help your grandpa.

Not fair!

Mothers were also very important to the ancient Egyptians. Even back then, there was a Mother's Day to honor them. There was also a celebration called mother's feast.

Respect Mom. She's the boss!

WALLS as Thin as Paper

There were no forests in ancient Egypt, so wood was hard to find. Houses were made from other **materials**, such as mud bricks. Some Egyptians built with papyrus. Yep—the same stuff they used to make paper.

This really is a full house!

Most houses had only three rooms. There was a bedroom, a kitchen, and a living room. Remember all those family members living together? They could be sharing one bedroom!

Want a comfy couch in ancient Egypt? They were more about practicality. Furniture might be built *into* the house. The chairs and tables could be part of the walls!

I am important.

Some wealthy ancient Egyptians had separate chairs. These chairs were different sizes. The most important people would sit on the highest chairs.

But I am VERY important.

Now, where did I bury that frozen yogurt?

What about the kitchen? Your food might take twice as long to cook since ovens were made of stone. There weren't any fridges, either. Ancient Egyptians dug pits in the ground to keep food cool.

FISHY Food and Drinks

Thirsty? In ancient Egypt, there weren't soda machines or lemonade stands. But there was water—the Nile was right there! Unfortunately, its water was not safe to drink. Instead, people often made a drink from a kind of grain called barley.

I think it's time to sell some magic beans for a cow!

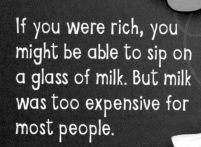

If you were rich, you might be able to sip on a glass of milk. But milk was too expensive for most people.

This is so dry.

Finding something good to eat could also be tricky in ancient Egypt. A lot of people could not afford meat, so they had bread and vegetables. And if you can't get milk, that means no cheese or butter, either.

Sometimes, people would eat fish from the Nile. However, fishing could be risky business. Some fish were considered **sacred**, so you might be in big trouble if you ate the wrong one!

I'm sacred! Don't eat me!

No, he's not! I am! Or I could be.

Eaten by THE GODS

Just as in several other **cultures**, the ancient Egyptians **worshipped** lots of gods and goddesses. And often, Egyptian gods didn't look quite ... human.

In fact, ancient Egyptian gods might look strange to you today. Many were similar to people and walked on two legs. But some gods also had the heads of one kind of creature and the bodies of another!

These gods are awesome!

If you wanted something from one of these gods, you had to ask the **temple** gods. They would pass your message on to the right god. If you didn't get what you wanted, you could visit the temple and give its god statue a whack! This showed you were not happy.

WHACK!

OUCH!

Are you being good? Because I'm watching . . .

Some gods were scary. Ammit had a frightening crocodile head with sharp teeth. Many believed if you did something really bad in life, Ammit would appear in the **afterlife** to eat you.

Horrible HAIRSTYLES

Have you ever gotten a bad haircut? Well, you might not be a fan of the salons in ancient Egypt.

You'll love this latest style!

Kids in ancient Egypt often had a haircut called the sidelock of youth. For this look, you would shave your entire head except for one braid of hair on the side.

Who came up with this style?

You might think focusing on your clothes would help you forget your haircut. Well, you might not be wearing any! Children rarely wore clothes because of how hot it could get in Egypt.

Can I go outside now?

Children did, however, wear lots of jewelry, such as earrings, bracelets, and decorative bands. Sometimes, kids also wore **amulets** or had **symbols** on their clothes. People believed these helped protect children.

SPLINTERS
and Bones

No video games??

In ancient Egypt, there were no colorful, plastic toys. And there weren't any **electronics** either. So, what did children play with?

They had toys made from wood. There were wood dice, games, toy animals, and even dolls. Watch out for splinters!

Where's the fun in splinters?

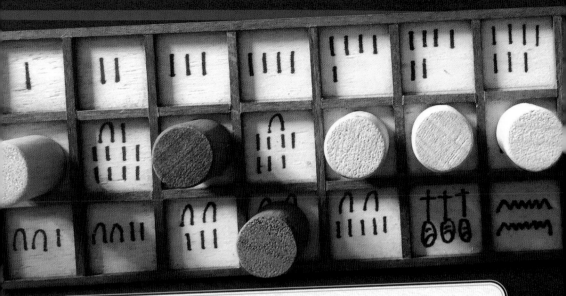

One board game in ancient Egypt was called Senet. Its board had 30 squares, and each player had 5 playing pieces. The first person to get all of their pieces off the board was the winner.

To find out how many spaces you could move in Senet, you had to throw sticks...or bones! You might want to get used to playing games with bones in ancient Egypt. They were easier to find than dice!

Gross! I don't want to play anymore!

Writing in
PICTURES

Most kids in ancient Egypt didn't go to school. Instead, they learned at home.

Children usually started school when they were about four. They were mainly taught by their parents, so let's hope yours know their stuff! Kids mostly learned how to do jobs.

But I'm trying my hardest!

Often, boys would learn the family trade. That means they would be doing the same job as their parents, usually their fathers. Boys were expected to take over these jobs one day. If a boy failed to do the job well, he might be sent away!

Some girls trained to become doctors or dentists. However, most learned how to take care of the home. This included knowing how to cook and sew. Sometimes, they also learned to take care of the family business.

My brother got sent away, so now I have to do his job!

I'm not sure I can read this shopping list!

Hieroglyphs

Many kids were taught to read and write as well as do basic math. However, writing in ancient Egypt was different than today. Ancient Egyptians used hieroglyphic writing.

This writing used hieroglyphs, or pictures, instead of letters. The pictures weren't always written from side to side like the words you're reading right now. In ancient Egypt, words could also be written going down a page.

L I K E

T H I S

To practice writing, Egyptian kids would use different tools than what you use in class now. Pens and pencils didn't exist then!

So, how am I supposed to write?

I don't think I'm very good at this.

Kids wrote on thick sheets of papyrus. They would use **reeds** dipped in ink to write with. Sounds messy!

GROWN UP

When?

Adulthood came early in ancient Egypt. Boys were adults at around 14, while girls were thought of as adults at around 12. That's pretty young to be done with having parents telling you what to do!

I never get to do what I want!

But even if your parents weren't telling you what to do, a lot of other people might be! Life in ancient Egypt was difficult. Only very rich people were able to do what they wanted.

An Egyptian girl was often married at 12 years old. She would leave her family to move in with her husband's. The new home could be just as crowded as the old one!

This new family is even bigger!

I don't want a job yet!

Kids in ancient Egypt usually began working at around 14, whether they wanted to or not. No more fun and games with wooden toys!

There were some seriously strange and difficult jobs in ancient Egypt. Unfortunately, you didn't have much say in your work!

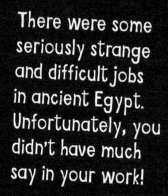

I wish my dad had a better job.

A scribe is a person whose job was to write things down. Maybe that's not such a bad job. But remember — scribes would write using hieroglyphs!

I forgot which word to use. Is it the bird or the lion?

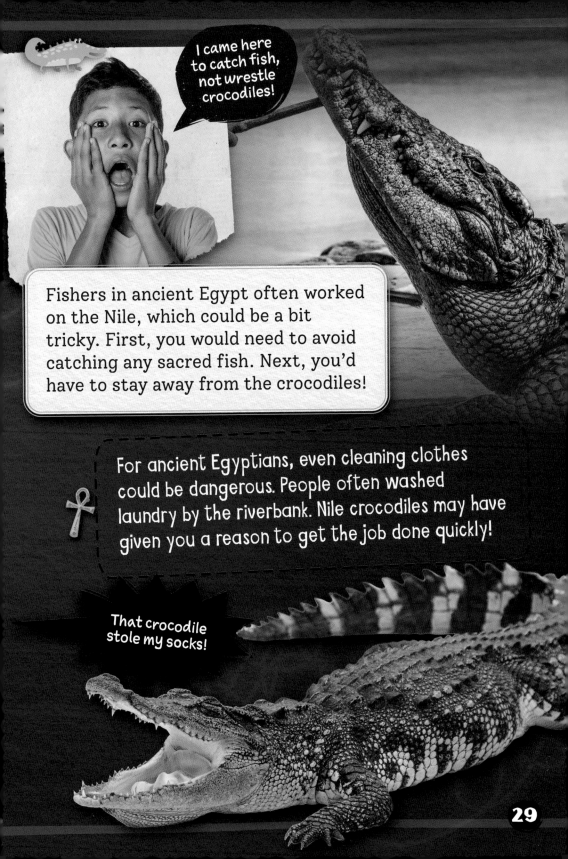

I came here to catch fish, not wrestle crocodiles!

Fishers in ancient Egypt often worked on the Nile, which could be a bit tricky. First, you would need to avoid catching any sacred fish. Next, you'd have to stay away from the crocodiles!

For ancient Egyptians, even cleaning clothes could be dangerous. People often washed laundry by the riverbank. Nile crocodiles may have given you a reason to get the job done quickly!

That crocodile stole my socks!

29

That's
TOUGH!

Do you still think being a kid today is tough? At least it's not nearly as tough as it was in ancient Egypt! From crocodile gods to bad haircuts, it was not a fun time to be a kid.

Which part of life in ancient Egypt sounds the toughest?

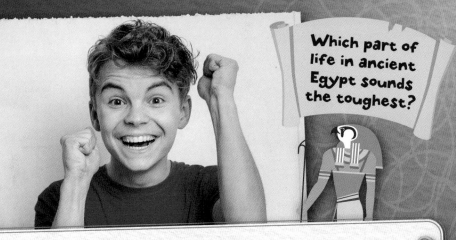

But don't worry. You're back in the present. You don't need to write in pictures, and no one will give you a sidelock of youth haircut . . . probably. So, get back to enjoying being a kid here and now!

GLOSSARY

afterlife the life of a person after he or she dies

amulets charms or decorations that are worn to protect against evil

civilization a large group of people that shares the same history and way of life

cultures the customs and traditions shared by a group of people

diseases illnesses

electronics devices, games, or equipment that work using electricity

materials substances used to build or make things

medicine something used or taken to fight off sickness or pain

natural made by nature

reeds tall, thin, woody plants

sacred holy or religious

scrolls rolls of papyrus used for writing

symbols things that stand in for other things

temple a building for religious practice

worshipped honored and respected as a god

woven made by crossing pieces of material over and under

INDEX

READ MORE

Finan, Catherine C. *Ancient Egypt (X–treme Facts: Ancient History).* Minneapolis: Bearport Publishing, 2022.

Reynolds, Donna. *Ancient Egypt Revealed (Unearthing Ancient Civilizations).* New York: Cavendish Square Publishing, 2023.

LEARN MORE ONLINE

1. Go to **www.factsurfer.com** or scan the QR code below.
2. Enter "**Tough Times Egypt**" into the search box.
3. Click on the cover of this book to see a list of websites.